Understanding the Death of a Loved One

WRITTEN BY

Bobbie Mercer

© Copyright 2016, Bobbie Mercer

All Rights Reserved.

No part of this book may be reproduced, stored in a retrieval system, or transmitted by any means, electronic, mechanical, photocopying, recording, or otherwise, without written permission from the author.

ISBN: 978-1-60414-899-2

So you've lost someone
that you love,
and you're finding it
hard to understand...

Feeling sad is a natural emotion, and it's okay to cry.

In fact, Jesus cried when he heard about the death of his friend Lazarus.

John 11:35 says, "Jesus wept."

Sadness and crying are normal responses to death, and so is fear.

Fear emerges because we don't understand death, or why our loved one had to die. But this fear is a negative emotion that does not come from God.

The bible gives us instructions for when this fear comes.

Psalm 56:3-4 says, "When I am afraid, I put my trust in you."

When we get scared and just don't understand, we must look to God for help, and trust that he will take care of us.

You may want to talk, hug, and be close to the person that passed away, but this is no longer possible.

I know you will miss them, but I hope this book will help you understand death and how to cope with the loss of a loved one.

So what is death anyway?

Death simply means the end of life. Death occurs when we lose the use of all vital body functions such as, our heartbeat, spontaneous breathing, and brain activity.

God made us to need all the parts of the body to live. We need our heart, lungs, liver, kidneys, brain and other body parts. If any or all of these body parts stop working properly, we can become sick and die.

Our bodies are like balloons. When a balloon is filled with air you can bounce and play with it. Over time, the balloon loses air, or it pops, and it is no longer functional. The same is true when we stop breathing, the air leaves our body and we can no longer function, so we die.

When a person dies, we take the time to remember them with a funeral.

A funeral is a way for everyone who knew and loved a person to celebrate their life. Family and loved ones come together to pray, say goodbye, celebrate, and share fond memories of the one whose passed away. Though you may not see that person again, your memory of them can never be taken away. You can remember their laugh, touch, smell, and smile in your heart and your mind forever.

Why does death happen?

Death is a part of life. It's a natural occurrence, like the changing of seasons, or rain falling from the sky. We may not enjoy rainy days, but they are necessary and a part of life.

Ecclesiastes 3:2 says, there is a time to be born and a time to die…

This simply means death is something we will all have to come in contact with sooner or later. We may not know when, we may not know why, but we do know it happens, so it's important to enjoy our lives, and the lives of the people God has placed around us.

People of all ages die for many different reasons, including accidents like storms, and earthquakes, illness, or by giving their lives for others, like soldiers, policeman and firefighters sometimes have to do. Most of the time, people die from old age, as their bodies get tired, weak, and simply wear out.

The cause of death is not as important as knowing how to deal with the loss of a loved one.

If you follow these simple rules, it will really help you to cope when you experience the death of a loved one.

Pray…ask God to give you and your family strength and comfort during this time.

Love…give and receive lots of hugs and kisses. Everyone needs to feel love when they've experienced loss.

Remember…try to focus on what a blessing it was to have that person in your life. Thank God for the time you shared.

Here is how some friends, learned to understand and accept the loss of someone they loved:

Bobbie's Story

One morning my sister and I were awakened by our dad, who was crying. He looked very sad, and couldn't stop shaking. As he reached out his hands, we hugged him tightly. Through the tears, he finally told us that mommy went to heaven. We felt sad and began to cry. We knew Mommy had been sick, and was in a lot of pain. But daddy told us that she was no longer in pain, which made us feel a little better. We <u>prayed</u> and asked God to bless Mommy, and help us deal with losing her. We <u>hugged</u> each other closely and somehow knew we would be all right.

As a family, we always went to church. We knew Mommy loved Jesus, and had gone to heaven to be with Him. Dad told us that one day we would all see her again in heaven and even though we will miss her hugs, her smile and her tender touch, we will still always <u>remember</u> her and how much she loved us.

Understanding the Death of a Loved One

Christina's Story

Mom arrived to pick me up from piano class. We were in a hurry because Mom had to pick up my brother, Anthony, from band practice. Mom and I were talking when her cell phone rang. Mom reached in her purse to answer it and out of nowhere appeared this school bus, which was running through a red light! Mom crashed into the bus on the left side, the bus tipped over and we were trapped underneath. All I heard was a loud bang and glass breaking. After Mom's car came to a stop, we were both unable to move. I was praying, crying and bleeding

at the same time. I thought my mom was dead, because she wasn't moving! People were running from everywhere, coming to help, and I could hear screams from all around.

The bus had 30 children on it, and two girls were thrown from a window and died. My mom was very badly injured, and I had two broken legs. After arriving at the hospital, Mom and I were told the news about the deaths of the two little girls, and we were very sad. We <u>prayed</u> for the families of the little girls, and we even went to their funerals. I <u>hugged</u> both of the little girls' moms, and told them we were very sorry for their loss. I'll always <u>remember</u> those little girls, and I often pray for them before I go to sleep.

My Story

One afternoon, Mom, my dog Bosco, and I went to the pet center to buy his food. I got out of the truck but before I could close the door, Bosco jumped out and was hit by a car. I ran to him, and tried to pick him up but he was too heavy for me. Two men ran over to help me get him into the doctor's office. Bosco never opened his eyes.

The animal doctor looked very sad as he handed me Bosco's collar, and then he <u>prayed</u> for me. My best friend had died, and I did not get to say goodbye to him. I cried for a long time, because I missed him.

All my parents' <u>hugs and kisses</u> were nice, but it didn't stop the pain. When someone we love dies, it hurts because we know that we won't see them again.

A few days after Bosco was buried, Mom and Dad surprised me with a brand new puppy! I named him Socks because he was all black but his paws were snow white and it looked like he was wearing socks. I also thought Socks was a good name because I <u>remembered</u> how Bosco used to always steal my socks!

Though I still missed Bosco, I was happy to have a new puppy to love.

What happens when you die?

When a person dies, their spirit leaves their body and flies away like a bird, while their body is left on earth to be buried.

Your spirt is eternal, which means it never dies. We are made in God's image and likeness. God is a spirit, and so are we. The difference is, we live on earth and God lives in heaven.

While on earth, we need a body for our spirit to live in, or else we would be a ghost! We need bodies so people on earth can hear, see and touch us. When a person dies, their spirit goes to heaven to be judged by God. If you have accepted Jesus Christ as the Lord of your life, your spirit will enter heaven.

2 Corinthians 5:8 says, "And we are not afraid but are quite content to die, for then we will be at home with the Lord."

Death is not as sad when you're in Christ, and you have properly prepared for death.

I remember when I heard the news of my brother passing away. I started to cry and felt sad but then I remembered, my brother had accepted Jesus Christ as his Lord, which meant he was now in a better place because he prepared for death.

How do you prepare for death?

Death can come at any time. No one knows exactly when they are going to die, but you can still prepare. We prepare for death by knowing and accepting Jesus Christ as the Lord and savior of our lives. When Jesus is your Lord, and you have received him in your heart, death is not as painful or scary. It's like moving from one house to another, or going from one grade to the next, but instead of changing houses or grades, you're moving from earth to heaven! Heaven is a much better, safer, cleaner, cooler place!

Heaven has streets of gold, huge mansions, friendly animals, beautiful angels, sparkling jewels, and most importantly, Jesus lives there!

Jesus made it possible for everyone to make it into heaven when he died for the sins of the world. He gave his life for us! He saved us, because he wanted us to experience Him, and all the wonderful things He promised. Salvation and eternal life with Him is a promise.

Do you know Jesus Christ as your savior? If you have not already accepted Jesus into your heart, please say this prayer.

> *"Father, I believe that Jesus is the son of God, I believe that he died on the cross for my sins, I believe that he was buried and rose again, and is now seated in heaven. I accept Jesus Christ as the Lord of my life. Please forgive me for my sins, and cleanse me. I give you my life. Come and live in my heart today, in Jesus' Name, Amen."*

www.ingramcontent.com/pod-product-compliance
Lightning Source LLC
Chambersburg PA
CBHW061226070526
44584CB00029B/4008